Better Homes and Ga

Kids' Party Cook Book

Our seal assures you that every recipe in *Kids' Party Cook Book*
has been tested in the Better Homes and Gardens® Test Kitchen.
This means that each recipe is practical and reliable, and
meets our high standards of taste appeal.

BETTER HOMES AND GARDENS® BOOKS

Editor: Gerald M. Knox
Art Director: Ernest Shelton
Managing Editor: David A. Kirchner
Copy and Production Editors: Marsha Jahns,
    Mary Helen Schiltz, Carl Voss, David A. Walsh

Food and Nutrition Editor: Nancy Byal
Department Head, Cook Books: Sharyl Heiken
Associate Department Heads: Sandra Granseth,
    Rosemary C. Hutchinson, Elizabeth Woolever
Senior Food Editors: Julia Malloy, Marcia Stanley,
    Joyce Trollope
Associate Food Editors: Barbara Atkins, Linda Foley,
    Linda Henry, Lynn Hoppe, Jill Johnson, Mary Jo Plutt,
    Maureen Powers, Martha Schiel
Recipe Development Editor: Marion Viall
Test Kitchen Director: Sharon Stilwell
Test Kitchen Photo Studio Director: Janet Pittman
Test Kitchen Home Economists: Jean Brekke,
    Kay Cargill, Marilyn Cornelius, Jennifer Darling,
    Maryellyn Krantz, Lynelle Munn, Dianna Nolin,
    Marge Steenson, Cynthia Volcko

Associate Art Directors: Linda Ford Vermie,
    Neoma Alt West, Randall Yontz
Assistant Art Directors: Lynda Haupert,
    Harijs Priekulis, Tom Wegner
Senior Graphic Designers: Alisann Dixon,
    Mike Eagleton, Lyne Neymeyer, Stan Sams
Graphic Designers: Mike Burns, Sally Cooper, Jack Murphy,
    Darla Whipple-Frain, Brian Wignall, Kimberly Zarley

Vice President, Editorial Director: Doris Eby
Executive Director, Editorial Services: Duane L. Gregg

Senior Vice President, General Manager: Fred Stines
Director of Publishing: Robert B. Nelson
Vice President, Retail Marketing: Jamie Martin
Vice President, Direct Marketing: Arthur Heydendael

KIDS' PARTY COOK BOOK

Editor: Mary Jo Plutt
Copy and Production Editor: Mary Helen Schiltz
Graphic Designer: Alisann Dixon
Electronic Text Processor: Donna Russell
Contributing Photographers: Mike Dieter, Jim Hedrich
Food Stylist: Janet Pittman
Contributing Illustrator: Thomas Rosborough

Muppet characters on page 60 are used by permission of Children's
Television Workshop. Copyright © 1985 Muppets, Inc.

On the cover: Teddy Bear Cake, Raspberry Twinkle, Glazed
Sunflower Nuts (See recipes, pages 20 and 21.)

Contents

Tis the Season

TEDDY
· BEAR ·
PARTY

we're having
SLUMBER

You're Invited . . .

The invitations are out and you're invited to a fun-filled party for kids. Just browse through this book and gather dozens of imaginative ideas to help make the next party for your child a wonderful time. Here you'll find kid-approved party foods ranging from one-of-a-kind decorated cakes and cookies to fun-to-eat main dishes. And because we realize that the food is only the first step to a successful party, we've included plenty of tips for invitations, decorations, and games.

So pick up your pencil, turn the page, and start jotting down ideas for your next kids' party. It's sure to please pint-size partygoers.

Hot Milk Sponge Cake

1 cup all-purpose flour 1 teaspoon baking powder ¼ teaspoon salt	● Grease and lightly flour a 9x9x2-inch baking pan. Set aside. In a small mixing bowl stir together flour, baking powder, and salt.	A sponge cake has a firmer texture than a butter cake, so it crumbs less. This makes it easier to frost. That's why we used it for *Mr. Giggles* (see recipe, page 13).
2 eggs 1 cup sugar	● In small mixer bowl beat eggs with an electric mixer on high speed about 4 minutes or till thick. Gradually add sugar and beat on medium speed for 4 minutes more, scraping bottom and sides of bowl occasionally. Add flour mixture to egg mixture and stir just till blended.	
½ cup milk 2 tablespoons butter *or* margarine	● In a small saucepan heat milk with butter or margarine till butter melts. Stir into batter and mix well. Turn batter into pan. Bake in a 350° oven for 20 to 25 minutes or till done. Cool in pan for 10 minutes. Remove from pan. Cool completely. Serves 9.	

Yellow Cake

2-LAYER-SIZE CAKE		1-LAYER-SIZE CAKE
2¾ cups all-purpose flour 2½ teaspoons baking powder ½ teaspoon salt	● Grease and lightly flour baking pan(s). For 2-layer-size cake, use two 8x1½-inch or 9x1½-inch round baking pans, *or* one 13x9x2-inch baking pan. For 1-layer-size cake, use one 8x1½-inch or 9x1½-inch round baking pan, *or* one 8x8x2-inch baking pan. Set aside. In a small mixing bowl stir together the flour, baking powder, and salt.	1⅓ cups all-purpose flour 1¼ teaspoons baking powder ¼ teaspoon salt
½ cup butter *or* margarine 1¾ cups sugar 1½ teaspoons vanilla	● In a mixer bowl beat butter or margarine with an electric mixer till softened (about 30 seconds). Add sugar and vanilla. Beat till well combined.	¼ cup butter *or* margarine ¾ cup sugar ¾ teaspoon vanilla

2 eggs
1¼ cups milk
	● Add egg(s), one at a time, beating for 1 minute after each. Alternately add flour mixture and milk to beaten mixture, beating on low speed after each addition just till combined.
	    Turn batter into the prepared pan(s). Bake in a 350° oven for 30 to 35 minutes for all cake sizes or till done.
	    Cool cake(s) in pan(s) for 10 minutes. If desired, remove cake(s) from pan(s), then cool completely. A 2-layer-size cake makes 12 to 15 servings and a 1-layer-size cake makes 6 to 8 servings.
		1 egg
		⅔ cup milk

Chocolate Cake

2-LAYER-SIZE CAKE		1-LAYER-SIZE CAKE
2 cups all-purpose flour 2 cups sugar 1 teaspoon baking soda ½ teaspoon salt	● Grease and lightly flour baking pan(s). For a 2-layer-size cake, use two 8x1½-inch or 9x1½-inch round baking pans, *or* one 13x9x2-inch baking pan. For a 1-layer-size cake, use one 8x1½-inch or 9x1½-inch round baking pan, *or* one 8x8x2-inch baking pan. Set aside. 　In a mixer bowl stir together flour, sugar, baking soda, and salt.	1 cup all-purpose flour 1 cup sugar ½ teaspoon baking soda ¼ teaspoon salt
1 cup butter *or* margarine 1 cup water ⅓ cup unsweetened cocoa powder	● In a small saucepan combine butter or margarine, water, and cocoa powder. Bring just to boiling, stirring constantly. Remove from heat. Add cocoa mixture to flour mixture. Beat with an electric mixer on low speed just till combined.	½ cup butter *or* margarine ½ cup water 3 tablespoons unsweetened cocoa powder
2 eggs ½ cup buttermilk *or* sour milk 1½ teaspoons vanilla	● Add egg(s), buttermilk or sour milk, and vanilla, then beat on low speed for 1 minute. (Batter will be thin.) 　Turn batter into the prepared pan(s). Bake in a 350° oven till done: 25 to 30 minutes for 8- or 9-inch round layer(s), or an 8-inch-square cake; 30 to 35 minutes for a 13x9-inch cake. 　Cool cake(s) in the pan(s) for 10 minutes. If desired, remove cake(s) from pan(s), then cool completely. A 2-layer-size cake makes 12 to 15 servings and a 1-layer-size cake makes 6 to 8 servings.	1 egg ¼ cup buttermilk *or* sour milk 1 teaspoon vanilla

Easy Cupcakes

Make every party guest feel special with his or her very own little decorated cake. To make cupcakes, use either the *Yellow Cake* or *Chocolate Cake* recipe. Grease and lightly flour 2½-inch muffin pans or line with paper bake cups. Then fill each cup half full with batter. Bake the cakes in a 350° oven about 20 minutes or until a wooden toothpick inserted in the center comes out clean.

Cool the cakes in the pans for 5 minutes. Remove them from the pans, then cool completely on a wire rack. Plan on a 2-layer-size cake making about 24 cupcakes and a 1-layer-size cake making about 12.

After the cakes are cooled, frost them with either *Butter Frosting* or *Chocolate Butter Frosting* (see recipes, page 8). If desired, sprinkle each cake with chopped nuts, crushed hard candies, or miniature semisweet chocolate pieces.

Butter Frosting

2 CUPS		1 CUP
6 tablespoons butter *or* margarine **4½ to 4¾ cups sifted powdered sugar**	● In a small mixer bowl beat butter or margarine with an electric mixer on medium speed till light and fluffy. Gradually add about *half* of the powdered sugar, beating well.	**3 tablespoons butter *or* margarine** **2¼ to 2½ cups sifted powdered sugar**
¼ cup milk **1½ teaspoons vanilla**	● Beat in milk and vanilla. Gradually beat in the remaining powdered sugar. Then beat in additional milk, if necessary, to make frosting spreadable.	**2 tablespoons milk** **¾ teaspoon vanilla**

Chocolate Butter Frosting

2 CUPS		1 CUP
2 squares (2 ounces) unsweetened chocolate **6 tablespoons butter *or* margarine** **4½ to 4¾ cups sifted powdered sugar**	● In a small heavy saucepan melt chocolate over low heat, stirring often. Cool slightly. Meanwhile, in a small mixer bowl beat butter or margarine with an electric mixer on medium speed till light and fluffy. Gradually add about *half* of the powdered sugar, beating well.	**1 square (1 ounce) unsweetened chocolate** **3 tablespoons butter *or* margarine** **2¼ to 2½ cups sifted powdered sugar**
¼ cup milk **1½ teaspoons vanilla**	● Beat in milk, vanilla, and chocolate. Gradually beat in remaining powdered sugar. Then beat in additional milk, if necessary, to make frosting spreadable.	**2 tablespoons milk** **¾ teaspoon vanilla**

The Finishing Touch

For dots and stars, hold the decorating bag at a 90-degree angle.

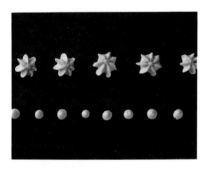

With the star or writing tip almost touching the cake, squeeze out frosting to form a star or dot. Stop squeezing, then lift off.

With just a few hints and a little practice, you can learn to decorate truly show-stopping party cakes.

● The easiest frosting to use for decorating is a buttercream frosting (see recipes, opposite). And for best results, make sure the frosting is at the right consistency by following this rule-of-thumb. For piped designs, the frosting should be slightly stiffer than it is for spreading. (The frosting should be able to hold the shape of the design.) To make the frosting stiffer, stir in a little extra powdered sugar. To make it thinner, stir in a few drops of water.

● Color your frosting with paste food coloring instead of liquid food coloring because the paste food coloring will tint the frosting without thinning it. Start by adding only a small amount from the tip of a wooden toothpick. Then blend the coloring into the frosting and add a little more, if needed.

● You can choose from several different types of decorating bags. Reusable bags are made from cloth or plastic, and must be washed and dried each time you change a frosting color. Or, make your own disposable decorating bags from parchment paper. Just take a 12x12x17-inch parchment triangle and form a cone. Tape the outside seam to about 1 inch from the tip. Then snip off ½ to ¾ inch from the tip, depending on the size of your decorating tip.

To use the bag or cone, drop the decorating tip into the bag. Half-fill the bag with frosting. Fold in the top corners, then fold the top down to meet the frosting level.

● Although there are many different types of decorating tips available, we've used only the medium-size writing and star tips in this book. The writing tip is used for making lines, dots, and for writing, as shown. And the star tip is used for making stars and zigzag borders, also shown.

To make lines, to write, or to make zigzag borders, hold the bag at a 45-degree angle.

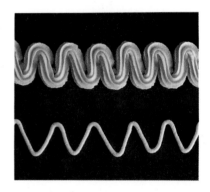

For a zigzag border, touch the star tip to the cake and move the tip from side to side.

For lines or writing, guide the writing tip just above the cake as you squeeze. To end the line, gently touch the tip to the cake, stop squeezing, then lift off.

Making a Special Cake

Whether your cake is from scratch or a mix, follow these hints for light, tender results.
● You'll find that the ingredients will mix more easily if you let the butter or margarine, eggs, and milk set out at room temperature about an hour before mixing.
● For evenness in baking, place the cake pans as near to the center of the oven as possible without touching each other so the hot air will move freely around the cakes. If the pans won't fit on one shelf, stagger them on two shelves. Don't put them directly under each other.
● Test for doneness by inserting a wooden toothpick into the center of the cake layer. If the toothpick doesn't come out clean, continue baking a few minutes more, then test again.
● Cool the cakes in the pans on wire racks for 10 minutes. Then, with a knife, loosen the edges from the pans. To remove each cake layer, place a wire rack on top of the cake pan. Invert rack and pan, then lift off the pan. Don't let the cakes cool in the pans for more than 10 minutes or they might stick.

Place a second wire rack upside down on top of the cake layer and invert it again, so the bottom rests on the rack. Finish cooling the cakes before frosting.

Drum Cake

4 cups creamy white frosting *(use Butter Frosting on page 8 or 2 creamy white frosting mixes for a 2-layer cake)* **Yellow paste food coloring** **Red paste food coloring**	● Tint about ¾ *cup* of the frosting with yellow paste food coloring and set aside. Tint *half* of the remaining frosting with red paste food coloring and set aside.	Cut out each "come be in our band" invitation in the shape of a musical note. Attach it to a kazoo, toy flute, or bell. Ask your guests to practice up before the day of the party. Then, at the party, have a parade and serve this musical cake.
3 8- *or* **9-inch round baked cake layers** *(use a recipe on page 6 or 7, or a 1- and 2-layer-size cake mixes)*	● Level *one* cake layer by using a sharp knife to cut a thin slice from its top. Assemble cake by placing another cake layer, top side down, on a serving plate. Spread with *one-third* of the white frosting. Place the leveled cake layer, cut side down, on frosted layer, making sure edges are aligned. Spread with another *one-third* of the white frosting. Add third cake layer, top side up, making sure the edges are aligned.	
Star decorating tip **Decorating bag**	● Frost sides of cake with red-tinted frosting. Then frost top of cake with remaining white frosting. Use the star tip, decorating bag, and yellow-tinted frosting to pipe a star border around the top and bottom edges of cake. Use star tip and yellow-tinted frosting to pipe joining diagonal lines, at 3-inch intervals, from top to bottom of cake.	
7 to 10 small green gumdrops, cut lengthwise in half	● Press gumdrop halves into top and bottom edges of cake where diagonal lines meet.	
2 ball-shape lollipops	● For drumsticks, cross lollipops on top of cake. Makes 12 to 16 servings.	

Make-Ahead Baked Alaska

1 8-inch-square baked cake
(use a recipe on page 6 or 7, or a 1-layer-size cake mix)
5 3-ounce chocolate-covered vanilla ice cream bars

● Cool cake in pan for 10 minutes. Remove cake from pan, then cool completely.

Cut a 10-inch-square piece of foil; place foil on baking sheet. Place cake onto center of foil.

Remove sticks from ice cream bars and arrange bars on cake to cover surface to within ½ inch of cake's edge. Place cake and ice cream in freezer.

4 egg whites
¼ teaspoon vanilla
⅛ teaspoon salt
½ cup sugar

● Preheat the oven to 500°.

Meanwhile, for meringue, in a large mixer bowl beat egg whites, vanilla, and salt with an electric mixer on medium speed about 1 minute or till soft peaks form (tips curl).

Gradually add the sugar, about 1 tablespoon at a time. Continue beating with the electric mixer on high speed about 7 minutes more or till the mixture forms stiff, glossy peaks (tips stand straight) and sugar is dissolved.

● Remove cake and ice cream from freezer. Quickly spread meringue over sides and top of cake and ice cream, carefully sealing to edge of foil with meringue. Swirl top with back of spoon to form a decorative pattern.

Bake in the 500° oven for 2 to 3 minutes or till meringue is light brown. Return cake to freezer and freeze. (Freeze for no more than 5 hours.)

● To serve, use two spatulas to lift cake from foil to a cold serving platter. Cut into squares with a sharp knife. Serves 9.

When you don't have a platter large enough for your cake, make a foil-covered cake board.

First cut a piece of heavy cardboard 1 to 2 inches larger than the cake. Then cut the foil about 3 inches larger than the cardboard. To make the foil fit neatly around the curved edges of the board, snip or tear slits at 1- to 1½-inch intervals. Fold the edges of the foil around the cardboard and tape to the underside.

Mr. Giggles

Batter for Hot Milk Sponge Cake (use recipe on page 6) 	● Grease and lightly flour 2 oven-proof 1-quart glass mixing bowls. Divide batter between the prepared bowls.
	Bake in a 350° oven about 35 minutes or till done. Cool cakes in the bowls for 10 minutes. Remove cakes from bowls, then cool completely.
	Level top of cakes by using a sharp knife to cut a thin slice from each top.
2 cups creamy white frosting (use Butter Frosting on page 8 or a creamy white frosting mix for a 2-layer cake)	● Spread the cut side of one cake with some of the frosting and top with the other cake, cut side down. Frost entire cake with the remaining frosting.
2 cups creamy white frosting (use Butter Frosting on page 8 or a creamy white frosting mix for a 2-layer cake) **Red paste food coloring** **Yellow paste food coloring** **Blue paste food coloring** **Star decorating tip** **Decorating bag** **Writing decorating tip**	● Tint 1¼ cups of the frosting with red paste food coloring, ½ cup with yellow coloring, and ¼ cup with blue coloring. Use the star tip, decorating bag, and red-tinted frosting to pipe stars on cake for hair. Change star tip to writing tip and pipe lines for mouth and eyebrows. Using the writing tip and blue-tinted frosting, pipe lines for eyes. Using the star tip and yellow-tinted frosting, pipe 2 zigzag borders around base of cake for collar.
1 large red gumdrop **1 paper party hat** **Colored paper**	● Press gumdrop into frosting for nose. Place party hat on top of cake. (If hat is too big, adjust by restapling it.) Make a bow tie from paper. Makes 10 servings.

Mr. Giggles doesn't have to be the only clown at the party. Buy some theatrical makeup from a magic or costume rental shop, and paint a clown face on each child. You may need to ask a friend to help so the kids won't get impatient waiting. And don't forget to have a couple of mirrors on hand so the clowns will be able to giggle at themselves.

Spaceship Cake

1. **8- *or* 9-inch round baked cake layer** *(use a recipe on page 6 or 7, or a 1-layer-size cake mix)*

3. **cups creamy white frosting** *(use Butter Frosting on page 8 or creamy white frosting mixes for 1- and 2-layer cakes)*
   Blue paste food coloring
   Black paste food coloring

● Cut cake according to directions and as shown in diagram at right. To make frosting the cake easier, let cake stand for 1 to 2 hours or until the cut edges are slightly dry.

● Tint about ¾ *cup* of the frosting with blue paste food coloring. Set aside.
   Tint about ½ *cup* of the frosting with black paste food coloring and set aside.

● To assemble spaceship, join pieces together with some white frosting, as shown in diagram at right.
   Frost the bottom 2 inches of cake, including its sides, with blue-tinted frosting.
   Reserve ¼ *cup* of the white frosting. Frost remaining sides and top of cake with remaining white frosting.

Turn a round cake into a spaceship by following the diagram below. First, cut a 2-inch slice from the cake. Then cut the slice in half for the fins of the spaceship.
   To assemble the spaceship, attach the fins to the outside of the cake with some white frosting.

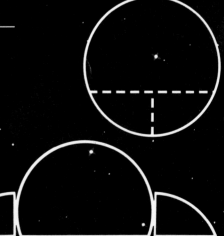

Writing decorating tip **Decorating bag**	● Use the writing tip, decorating bag, and black-tinted frosting to pipe a line across top of cake where the blue and white frosting meet. Pipe another line 1 inch above the first line and a third line on the bottom edge of the cake. Divide bottom half of spaceship into four sections by piping three lines from top black line to bottom of cake, curving the two outer lines, as shown.
1 roll red fruit-flavored **circle candies** **4 multicolored fruit-flavored** **circle candies**	● For rivets, use the writing tip and reserved white frosting to pipe dots next to black lines on blue portion of cake. Decorate cake with candies, as shown. If necessary, use white frosting to attach candies to cake.
4 red cinnamon candies **2 tiny marshmallows, cut** **in half** **2 vanilla wafers** **4 1½-inch pieces shoestring** **licorice** **4 small gumdrops**	● For martians, attach one cinnamon candy in center of each marshmallow half with some white frosting to make eyes. Attach eyes to cookies with some white frosting. Place martians on the top white portion of cake. For antennas, insert one piece of licorice into each gumdrop. Place antennas on cake right above each martian's head. Makes 6 to 8 servings.

At a space party, let the kids go on an imaginary journey by playing "Pin the Spaceship on the Planet."

Soda Fountain Cakes

12 **flat-bottom ice-cream cones**
   Batter for a 1-layer-size yellow cake *(use Yellow Cake on page 6 or a 1-layer-size golden yellow cake mix)*

● Place ice-cream cones in a muffin pan or large baking pan.
   Prepare cake batter as directed. Fill each cone to within 1 inch of top.
   Bake in a 350° oven about 30 minutes or till done. Remove cakes from pan, then cool completely.

1 **cup creamy white frosting** *(use Butter Frosting on page 8 or a creamy white frosting mix for a 1-layer cake)*
¼ **cup finely crushed hard candies, chopped nuts, *or* miniature semisweet chocolate pieces**
6 **8-inch plastic drinking straws**

● Frost top of cakes with frosting. Sprinkle candy, nuts, or chocolate pieces on the top of each cake.
   Cut each straw into 4 pieces. Insert 2 pieces into the top of each cake, as shown at right. Makes 12 cupcakes.

You won't find these great-tasting sodas at the ice cream parlor. Make them by baking the batter in ice-cream cones with flat bottoms and straight sides. Then decorate the tops with candy or nuts and straws.

Confetti Cupcakes

1 **8-ounce can crushed pineapple (juice pack)**
1 **16-ounce package pound cake mix**
½ **cup chopped red and green maraschino cherries**

● Grease and lightly flour muffin pans or line with paper bake cups. Set aside.
   Drain pineapple, reserving juice. Add enough water to juice to make ⅔ cup.
   Prepare cake mix according to package directions, *except* omit the water and stir in the reserved juice mixture. Stir in the pineapple and cherries. Fill each muffin cup two-thirds full.
   Bake in a 350° oven about 20 minutes or till done. Cool cupcakes in the pans for 5 minutes. Remove from pans, then cool completely.

Looking for birthday treats to send to school? These fruit-filled cupcakes are sure to be a hit with the kids.

   For easy packing, leave off the candles. Crush the candies and sprinkle some on top of each cupcake.

2 **cups creamy white frosting** *(use Butter Frosting on page 8 or a creamy white frosting mix for a 2-layer cake)*
22 **to 24 fruit-flavored circle candies**
22 **to 24 birthday candles**

● Frost top of cupcakes with frosting. Place one candy on top of each cake and insert a candle into the hole. Makes 22 to 24 cupcakes.

Bite-Size Wishes

½ cup miniature semisweet chocolate pieces
¼ cup chopped walnuts
2 tablespoons sugar

● For topping, in a small mixing bowl combine chocolate pieces, walnuts, and sugar. Set mixture aside.

Batter for a 1-layer-size cake *(use a recipe on page 6 or 7, or a 1-layer-size cake mix)*

● Grease and lightly flour 1¾-inch muffin pans or line the pans with paper bake cups.
   Prepare cake batter as directed. Fill each cup two-thirds full. (If you don't have enough small muffin pans, refrigerate the remaining batter while cupcakes bake. Or, for larger cupcake wishes, use 2½-inch muffin pans.)

● Sprinkle about *1 teaspoon* of topping mixture on top of each cupcake (1 tablepoon for larger cupcakes).
   Bake in a 350° oven about 12 minutes (about 20 minutes for larger cupcakes) or till done. Cool cupcakes in pans for 5 minutes. Remove from pans, then cool completely.

Make little party packages for each guest by wrapping each cake in plastic wrap. Bring up the edges of the wrap and, with ribbon, tie the wrap closed around the candle.

Birthday candles
Clear plastic wrap
Ribbon
Small plain self-adhesive labels

● Insert one candle into the center of each cupcake.
   Cut about thirty-six 6-inch-square pieces (or twelve 12x8-inch pieces for larger cupcakes) of clear plastic wrap. Place one cake in the center of each piece, then bring up edges. Tie closed with ribbon, as shown at right.
   Write a good wish or fortune on each label. Stick one label to the bottom of each cupcake package. Makes about 36 small or 12 large cupcakes.

Teddy Bear
Birthday Bash

Bring your teddy bear—we're having a party! Teddy bears
are definitely the favorite guests at this preschool party.
To develop your teddy bear theme, have your little host
or hostess help you put teddy bear stickers on
invitations, decorations, and party favors. During the
party, serve our Teddy Bear Cake and have each child tell
why their teddy bear is special. Then, wind up the party
with a teddy bear story. (See recipes, pages 20 and 21.)

MENU
Teddy Bear Cake
Ice Cream
Raspberry Twinkle
Glazed Sunflower Nuts

Teddy Bear Cake

Pictured on pages 18 and 19, and on the cover.

Batter for a 1-layer-size cake *(use a recipe on page 6 or 7, or a 1-layer-size cake mix)*	● Grease and lightly flour one 6-ounce custard cup *and* one 8x1½-inch or 9x1½-inch round baking pan. Fill the custard cup half full with batter and turn remaining batter into the pan. Bake in a 350° oven for 20 to 25 minutes or till done. Cool cake in the custard cup and in the pan for 10 minutes. Remove cake from custard cup and pan, then cool completely.

1 cup creamy white frosting *(use Butter Frosting on page 8 or a creamy white frosting mix for a 1-layer cake)*
1 cup flaked coconut
1 square (1 ounce) unsweetened chocolate, melted and cooled
	● Cut cupcake *horizontally* in thirds. For snout, attach the top cupcake slice to top of round cake with some frosting.
	    For ears, cut a ½-inch piece from each of the remaining cupcake slices and discard. Attach flat side of slices to edge of cake with some frosting.
	    Frost snout with some frosting, then sprinkle with some coconut.
	    Stir melted chocolate into remaining frosting. Frost sides, top, and ears of bear with the chocolate frosting.

½ square (½ ounce) unsweetened chocolate, melted and cooled	● Stir the remaining coconut into the melted chocolate. Sprinkle chocolate coconut around edge of ears and on chocolate frosting portion of face.
1 marshmallow, cut in half **1 large black gumdrop, cut crosswise in thirds** **Red shoestring licorice**	● Decorate face using marshmallow and two gumdrop slices for *eyes*, one gumdrop slice for nose, and licorice for mouth. Makes 6 to 8 servings.

MENU COUNTDOWN
1 day ahead:
Prepare and package Glazed Sunflower Nuts.
    Bake, cool, and wrap the cupcake and cake in clear plastic wrap.
Several hours ahead:
Decorate Teddy Bear Cake. Prepare, cover, and chill Raspberry Twinkle base.
Just before serving:
Stir carbonated beverage into raspberry base and pour into glasses.

You'll fall in love with this easy-to-make *Teddy Bear Cake* just as much as our young tasters did.

Raspberry Twinkle

Pictured on pages 18 and 19, and on the cover.

1 10-ounce package frozen red raspberries, partially thawed
¾ cup water

● In a blender container combine raspberries and water. Cover and blend till smooth. Chill till serving time.

1 10-ounce bottle (1¼ cups) lemon-lime carbonated beverage

● To serve, stir carbonated beverage into raspberry mixture. Pour into glasses. Makes 6 (4-ounce) servings.

This shimmery red drink is not only ideal for birthday parties, it can also brighten up Christmas or Valentine's Day festivities.

Glazed Sunflower Nuts

Pictured on pages 18 and 19, and on the cover.

½ cup sugar
1 tablespoon butter *or* margarine

● Line the bottom of a shallow baking pan with foil. Set pan aside.
  In a heavy 10-inch skillet combine sugar and butter or margarine. Cook over medium heat, stirring constantly, till sugar melts and turns a rich brown color.

1½ cups sunflower nuts

● Remove skillet from heat. Immediately add sunflower nuts. Stir to coat nuts evenly. Spread the mixture onto the prepared baking pan. Cool completely. Break mixture into clusters.

6 small clear plastic bags
Ribbon

● Package about ⅓ cup of the nuts in each bag. Tie closed with ribbon. Makes 6 (⅓-cup) servings.

Ribbons, streamers, and balloons all add to the party fun. Fill the balloons with helium and tie one to each chair. Then, when it's time to leave, each kid can take home the balloon from their chair.

Puppet Cookies

1⅓ cups butter *or* margarine ⅔ cup sugar	● In a large mixer bowl beat butter or margarine with an electric mixer on medium speed till softened (about 30 seconds). Add sugar and beat till fluffy.	**Everyone loves a puppet show. Divide your guests into groups of two or three. Then give each child some *Puppet Cookies* and let each group take turns putting on a show.**
½ teaspoon almond extract *or* 1 teaspoon vanilla 3⅓ cups all-purpose flour	● Add almond extract or vanilla, then beat well. With mixer on low speed, gradually add flour and beat till mixture resembles coarse crumbs.	
Desired food colorings	● Divide mixture into several parts, depending on the number of different colors you want. 　Add food coloring to each part, kneading with your hands till dough is smooth and color is mixed in.	
8 to 10 wooden sticks	● Form dough into puppet characters that are about ½ inch thick and 5 inches tall. Place cookies about 3 inches apart on ungreased cookie sheets. Carefully, insert a stick about 2 inches into the body portion of each cookie character.	**For our kid tasters, our Home Economists made the *Puppet Cookies* in the form of ducks, bunny rabbits, and pigs. They also made the storybook character Goldilocks and three bears.**
	● Bake in a 300° oven for 25 to 30 minutes or till edges are firm but bottoms are not brown. Cool completely on cookie sheet. Carefully remove cookies from sheet. Makes 8 to 10.	

Peachy-Keen Bars

1¼ cups all-purpose flour
¼ teaspoon baking powder
¼ teaspoon baking soda
¼ teaspoon salt
1 8-ounce can peach slices
   or crushed pineapple
   (juice pack)
	● Grease and lightly flour a 9x9x2-inch baking pan, then set pan aside.
	   In a small mixing bowl stir together flour, baking powder, soda, and salt. Set flour mixture aside.
	   Drain peaches or pineapple, reserving ⅓ *cup* syrup or juice. Chop peaches, then set peaches or pineapple aside.

⅓ cup sugar ¼ cup butter *or* margarine, softened	● In a small mixer bowl beat sugar and butter or margarine with an electric mixer on medium speed till fluffy.
1 egg ¼ teaspoon vanilla ½ cup coconut ¼ cup chopped walnuts	● Add egg and vanilla, then beat well. Add flour mixture and reserved syrup or juice alternately to egg mixture; beat till well blended. Stir in peaches or pineapple, coconut, and walnuts.
	● Spread dough into the prepared pan. Bake in a 350° oven for 30 to 35 minutes or till a wooden toothpick comes out clean. Cool completely in the pan on a wire rack.

2 tablespoons butter *or*
   margarine
1 cup sifted powdered sugar
2 teaspoons milk
½ teaspoon vanilla
	● Meanwhile, for frosting, in a small mixer bowl beat butter or margarine with an electric mixer on medium speed till softened. Gradually add about *half* of the powdered sugar, beating well. Beat in milk and vanilla. Gradually beat in the remaining powdered sugar, then additional milk, if necessary, to make frosting spreadable. Spread frosting on top of the bars.
	   If desired, place bars in a covered container and freeze. Thaw before serving. Makes 24 bars.

Keep these *Peachy-Keen Bars* on hand for a spur-of-the-moment party. They'll come in handy when kids need to wash away those rainy day blues. Just call up a few friends; pull out the crayons, paints, modeling clay, or board games; and pass around these yummy make-ahead bars.

Funny Faces

1 cup all-purpose flour
1 cup whole wheat flour
1 cup quick-cooking rolled
   oats
1 teaspoon baking soda
½ teaspoon ground
   cinnamon

● In a medium mixing bowl stir together flours, oats, baking soda, and cinnamon. Set flour mixture aside.

¾ cup butter *or* margarine
1 cup packed brown sugar
½ cup sugar

● In a large mixer bowl beat butter or margarine with an electric mixer on medium speed till softened (about 30 seconds). Add sugars. Beat till fluffy.

1 cup mashed bananas
   (about 3 medium)
1 egg
1 teaspoon vanilla
½ cup milk chocolate pieces
½ cup chopped peanuts

● Add bananas, egg, and vanilla, then beat well. Gradually add flour mixture and beat till well blended. Stir in chocolate pieces and peanuts.

Peanut butter *or*
   canned chocolate
   frosting
Assorted decorations
   (candy-coated milk
   chocolate pieces,
   miniature semisweet
   chocolate pieces, candy
   corn, fruit-flavored
   circle candies, nuts,
   gumdrops, shoestring
   licorice, jelly beans,
   tiny marshmallows,
   fruit leather,
   and/or chocolate
   caramel logs)

● For each cookie, drop about ¼ cup of dough onto greased cookie sheets. Spread dough into a 3-inch circles. Repeat with remaining dough, spacing the cookies 3 inches apart.

   Bake in a 350° oven for 12 to 15 minutes or till cookies are firm in center. Cool cookies on cookie sheet for 1 minute. Remove cookies from sheet to a wire rack, then cool completely.

   Frost cookies with peanut butter or frosting. Trim with assorted decorations to make faces. Makes about 18 cookies.

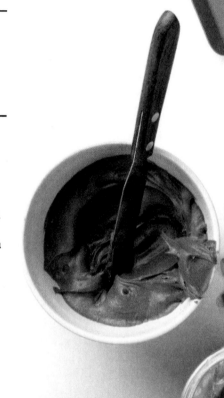

Celebration Cookie

1 15- *or* 16-ounce roll refrigerated double chocolate *or* chocolate chip cookie dough	● Cut *two-thirds* of the cookie dough roll into ½-inch-thick slices. Refrigerate the remaining dough and use as desired. On an ungreased cookie sheet arrange and press slices into an 8-inch circle.	**Highlight your party with this giant *Celebration Cookie.* It has all of the good flavors of chocolate, banana, and peanut butter rolled into one.**
	● Bake in a 400° oven for 10 to 15 minutes or till cookie is almost firm in center. Cool completely on cookie sheet.	
1 5-ounce can vanilla pudding ⅓ cup creamy peanut butter ¼ cup plain yogurt	● Meanwhile, in a small mixing bowl stir together vanilla pudding and peanut butter till smooth, then fold in yogurt. Up to 4 hours before serving, spread pudding mixture over top of cookie. Loosely cover and chill till serving time.	
1 medium banana, sliced 3 tablespoons chopped dry roasted peanuts (optional)	● At serving time, arrange banana slices on top of pudding mixture. If desired, sprinkle with peanuts. To serve, cut into wedges. Makes 6 servings.	

Frosty Cookiewiches

1 17-ounce roll refrigerated sugar cookie dough
Sherbet Filling, Pudding Filling, or Fruit 'n' Cheese Filling

● Slice and bake the cookie dough according to package directions.

Use one of the filling variations below to assemble the cookies into sandwiches.

Place cookie sandwiches on a baking sheet, then loosely cover and freeze till firm. If desired, wrap each sandwich in a 6-inch-square piece of foil and continue freezing till serving time. Makes 18.

Sherbet Filling: Spoon 1 quart of softened *orange, lemon, lime,* or *raspberry sherbet* into 3 clean 12-ounce juice cans or 10-ounce soup cans. Cover the open end of each can with foil and freeze till sherbet is firm.

To assemble cookies, remove the foil and other end from the sherbet-filled can. Press on one end, forcing sherbet roll out. With a sharp knife, cut sherbet roll into 6 slices. Place a slice between 2 cookies. Freeze as directed above.

● **Pudding Filling:** In a mixing bowl stir together one 17½-ounce can *chocolate pudding,* ½ cup toasted *coconut,* and ½ cup chopped *pecans.*

To assemble cookies, spread *half* of the cookies with the pudding mixture, using about 2 tablespoons for each. Top each with a second cookie. Freeze as directed above.

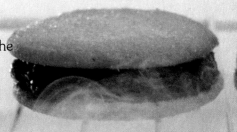

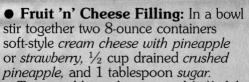

● **Fruit 'n' Cheese Filling:** In a bowl stir together two 8-ounce containers soft-style *cream cheese with pineapple* or *strawberry,* ½ cup drained *crushed pineapple,* and 1 tablespoon *sugar.*

To assemble cookies, spread *half* of the cookies with the mixture, using about 2 tablespoons for each. Top each with a second cookie. Freeze as directed above.

Trim-a-Tree Party

Holidays, cookies, and children—you can't ask for a better party combination. Whether it's Christmas, Thanksgiving, or Valentine's Day, the kids will love making an ornament for a holiday tree (see tip, page 30), or decorating a Cookie Tree to fit the season. To keep it simple, bake the cookies ahead. Then, when the guests arrive, just set out the decorating supplies and let the artists go to work. (See recipes, pages 30, 31, and 48.)

MENU
Make-an-Ornament Cookies *or*
Cookie Trees
Nutty-Nutbread Sandwiches
Holiday Nog

Make-an-Ornament Cookies

Pictured on pages 28 and 29.

2¼ **cups all-purpose flour** 2 **teaspoons baking powder** ½ **teaspoon ground nutmeg** **(optional)**	● In a small mixing bowl stir together flour; baking powder; and if desired, nutmeg. Set flour mixture aside.
½ **cup butter** *or* **margarine** 1 **cup sugar**	● In a large mixer bowl beat butter or margarine with an electric mixer on medium speed till softened (about 30 seconds). Add sugar and beat till fluffy.
1 **egg** 2 **tablespoons milk** ½ **teaspoon vanilla**	● Add egg, milk, and vanilla, then beat well. Gradually add flour mixture and beat till well blended. Cover and chill dough about 1 hour.
	● Roll out dough, half at a time, on a lightly floured surface to about ¼-inch thickness. Cut into desired shapes with cookie cutters or knife, rerolling dough as necessary. Transfer cookies to ungreased cookie sheets. With a plastic drinking straw, make one hole at top of each cookie.
	● Bake in a 375° oven for 8 to 10 minutes or till cookies are light brown around edges. While cookies are hot, if necessary, reopen holes with a toothpick. Remove cookies from sheet to a wire rack, then cool completely.
Assorted decorations (colored sugar, small multicolored decorative candies, *and/or* crushed hard candies) **Narrow ribbon** **Assorted tinted creamy white frostings*** *(use Butter Frosting on page 8 or a creamy white frosting mix)*	● Put assorted decorations in individual small plastic bowls. Tie a small piece of ribbon in the hole of each cookie for hanging. Let guests decorate the cookies by attaching the decorations to the cookies with some frosting. Let cookies stand about 30 minutes or till the frosting is slightly dry. Makes about 36 cookies. *For the directions on tinting frosting, see page 9.

MENU COUNTDOWN

1 day ahead:
Bake cookies and store in a covered container.

Several hours ahead:
For Make-an-Ornament Cookies, put decorative candies in small individual bowls. Make and cover frostings.

For Cookie Trees, dilute food coloring with water.

Prepare, cover, and chill Holiday Nog.

Prepare and wrap Nutty-Nutbread Sandwiches. (See recipe, page 48.)

During the party:
Set out the cookies and decorations, frostings, or food coloring mixtures.

Serve Nutty-Nutbread Sandwiches and Holiday Nog while guests are decorating cookies.

While the cookies are drying, keep the kids busy making other ornaments for your holiday tree. They can string popcorn, make paper chains, or cut out paper tree ornaments.

Christmas isn't the only time to decorate a tree. During the rest of the year, get a full-looking bare branch and stand it up in a pail of sand. Then make turkey, egg, or heart ornaments and have a Thanksgiving, Easter, or Valentine tree.

Cookie Trees

Dough for Make-an-Ornament Cookies *(use recipe on opposite page)*

● Prepare cookie dough as directed, *except* omit the nutmeg. Cover and chill dough about 1 hour.

Meanwhile, cut a paper pattern according to directions at right.

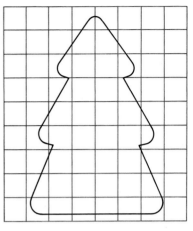

● Roll out dough, half at a time, on a lightly floured surface to about ¼-inch thickness. With a sharp well-floured knife, cut dough into tree shapes using the paper pattern. With a toothpick, mark the *center* of each cookie. Transfer cookies to greased cookie sheets.

With the knife, slash *half* of the cookies from the top of cookies to the center. Slash the remaining half of the cookies from the bottom of the cookies to the center.

To copy cookie tree, draw a 4x4½-inch rectangle. Divide it into ½-inch squares. Mark your grid exactly where the outline of the tree intersects each line on our grid. Connect marks. Cut out design.

● Bake in a 375° oven for 8 to 10 minutes or till cookies are light brown around edges. While cookies are hot, cut a ¼- to ⅜-inch-wide slot along slash. (Slots need to be as wide as cookies are thick.) Cool cookies on cookie sheet for 1 minute. Remove cookies from sheet to a wire rack, then cool completely.

Desired food colorings
Water
Artist paintbrushes

● Dilute ¼ *teaspoon* of each desired food coloring in *1 tablespoon* water.

Give each guest a bottom-slotted and a top-slotted cookie. Using paintbrushes and diluted food coloring, let guests paint designs onto the cookies.

When the cookies are dry, assemble the trees by slipping the bottom-slotted cookies into the top-slotted cookies to form three-dimensional trees. If necessary, trim slots to fit.

● Assemble trees, as shown at right. Makes about 8 trees.

Holiday Nog

5½ **cups milk**
 1 **package 4-serving-size** *instant* **French vanilla pudding mix**
 2 **tablespoons sugar**
 ¼ **teaspoon peppermint extract**

● In a blender container combine about *half* of the milk, pudding mix, sugar, and peppermint extract, then cover and blend till smooth. Pour into a large pitcher. Stir in the remaining milk. Cover and chill till serving time.

Crushed striped peppermint candy
 8 **striped peppermint candy sticks (optional)**

● To serve, stir and pour into glasses. Sprinkle with crushed candy. If desired, serve with peppermint sticks as stirrers. Makes 8 (6-ounce) servings.

Potato Flowers

6 medium potatoes (2 pounds) Shortening	● Scrub the potatoes, then rub with shortening. Prick several times with a fork. Bake potatoes in a 425° oven for 40 to 60 minutes or till tender. Cool potatoes until easy to handle. Cut a thin *lengthwise* slice from the top of each potato and discard the slice. Using a spoon, scoop out the inside of each potato, leaving ¼-inch-thick shell. Set potato shells aside.	**For a quick-and-easy party favor, serve each *Potato Flower* on a paper plate in a Frisbee.**
½ cup shredded American cheese (2 ounces) 1 tablespoon butter *or* margarine 1 teaspoon prepared mustard ⅛ teaspoon salt Dash pepper ½ cup dairy sour cream 2 tablespoons milk	● In a medium mixing bowl mash scooped-out potato pulp. Add cheese, butter or margarine, mustard, salt, and pepper, then stir till smooth and well combined. Stir in sour cream and milk. Mix well. Pile mixture into potato shells.	
5 to 6 frankfurters, sliced Paprika	● Overlap frankfurter slices on top of potato in a flowerlike fashion. Sprinkle with paprika. Loosely cover and chill till serving time.	**If you make the *Potato Flowers* right before serving, bake them immediately in a 400° oven for 8 to 10 minutes.**
	● To serve, remove cover from potatoes. Bake on an ungreased cookie sheet in a 350° oven for 25 to 30 minutes or till heated through. Makes 6 servings.	

Cheese Fun-Do

4 **medium carrots** 6 **ounces broccoli**	● Cut carrots into 2-inch sticks. Cut broccoli into flowerets, leaving 1-inch stems. Arrange vegetables around the edge of a large platter or tray, leaving room in the center. Cover and chill till serving time.

1 **16-ounce package frozen French-fried crinkle-cut potatoes**
1 **16-ounce package cheese spread, cut into 1-inch cubes**
2 **tablespoons milk**
	● To serve, prepare potatoes according to package directions.
	  Meanwhile, in a medium saucepan combine cheese spread and milk. Cook and stir over medium heat for 8 to 10 minutes or till heated through.
	  Pour cheese sauce into a large serving bowl with shallow sides. Place in center of the prepared platter. Add potatoes to edge of platter. Let guests dip vegetables into cheese dip. Makes 10 servings.

Just dip it and eat it! What could be an easier way to get the kids to eat their vegetables? Our kid tasters especially loved this cheese sauce on the crinkled french fries. If the sauce becomes too thick for easy dipping, just stir in more milk.

Here's The Answer

If you're a novice party giver, you'll probably have a few unanswered questions. To find the answers, we put ourselves in your shoes and asked:

Q. *What should I put on the invitations?*
A. Design the invitations to include the day, date, R.S.V.P., party beginning and ending times, and your name, address, and phone number.

Q. *What time of day should I have the party?*
A. Try scheduling a time when the kids will be at their best. For preschool kids, it's important that the party doesn't interfere with their nap schedule. And for older kids, although they might enjoy an after-school party, they may be too tired from the school day's activities. Weekends are better.

Q. *How can I prevent accidents?*
A. Take a few precautions before the party. Rearrange the furniture around the outside of the room and remove any small breakable objects from the party area.

Q. *How can I be sure my child will be a good host or hostess?*
A. Remind your child of good manners. For younger children, practice greeting guests at the door, accepting gifts graciously, and introducing guests who don't know each other.

Q. *How long should the party last?*
A. Limit your party to 1½ hours for 4- to 6-year-olds. And for older kids, a 2-hour party should be maximum.

Egg Heads

12 hard-cooked eggs ½ cup mayonnaise *or* salad dressing ½ teaspoon dry mustard ¼ teaspoon salt	● Cut eggs in half. Remove yolks and mash yolks with fork. Stir in mayonnaise or salad dressing, dry mustard, and salt. Continue mashing till mixture is smooth.	Give these *Egg Heads* "legs" by using paper rings as stands. To make the rings, cut twelve 6x1-inch strips of paper and fasten the ends together. Also cut out paper arms and stick them into the side of the eggs.

½ cup chopped nuts,
    cooked bacon pieces,
    finely shredded carrot
    or lettuce, finely
    shredded cheddar *or*
    American cheese,
    and/or pimiento pieces
	● Fill centers of egg whites with some of the yolk mixture. Then place egg halves back together using more of the yolk mixture as "glue."
	    For hair, attach nuts, bacon, carrot, lettuce, cheese, or pimiento to egg with some yolk mixture.	

Pitted ripe olives *and/or*
    pimiento-stuffed olives,
    cut into pieces
Pimiento pieces
Parsley sprigs (optional)
	● For eyes, nose, and mouth, attach olive and pimiento pieces to each egg with some yolk mixture. If desired, attach olive pieces and parsley for hats. Loosely cover. Chill till serving time. Makes 12.	

Spaghetti 'n' Cheese Haystacks

6 ounces spaghetti	● Break spaghetti into about 2-inch pieces. Cook spaghetti according to package directions. Drain and set aside.

2 tablespoons finely chopped onion
2 tablespoons finely chopped green pepper
1 tablespoon butter *or* margarine
1 tablespoon all-purpose flour
¼ teaspoon salt
Dash pepper
1¾ cups milk
8 ounces American cheese, cubed

● For cheese sauce, in a large saucepan cook onion and green pepper in butter or margarine till tender but not brown.

Stir in flour, salt, and pepper. Add milk all at once. Cook and stir till thickened and bubbly, then cook and stir for 1 minute more.

Add cheese cubes and stir till melted. Stir spaghetti into cheese sauce. Cover and chill till serving time.

8 4½-inch-diameter bologna slices

● To serve, in a large saucepan heat spaghetti mixture over medium heat till heated through, stirring occasionally.

Meanwhile, if necessary, peel casing from bologna slices. Cut each slice into quarters. Arrange pieces, as shown below, in eight 6-ounce custard cups.

Mound about ½ cup of heated spaghetti mixture in each cup and serve immediately. Makes 8 servings.

Hey, it's a party! Serve these cheese-sauced little haystacks at a hayride party. For added fun, play "Find the Almond in the Haystack" by placing one slivered almond in one of the bologna shells before filling it with the spaghetti mixture. At serving time, ask the kids to check their haystack for the almond. The one who finds the almond will be the lucky winner.

To save last-minute work, we chilled the spaghetti mixture, then reheated it. If you would rather serve it right after it's made, make the cheese sauce as directed, *except* use 2 tablespoons butter or margarine and 2 tablespoons flour.

To make the bologna cups, cut each slice of bologna into quarters. Then arrange the pieces, with pointed edges up, around the inside of the custard cups.

Fishettes

1 **medium potato, peeled and quartered**
2 **6½-ounce cans tuna, drained and flaked**
¼ **cup tartar sauce**
1 **tablespoon snipped parsley**
1 **teaspoon lemon juice**
 Salt
 Pepper

● In a small saucepan cook potato, covered, in boiling salted water about 15 minutes or till tender. Drain and mash potato (you should have about ¾ cup).
 Stir in tuna, tartar sauce, parsley, and lemon juice. Season to taste with salt and pepper.

● Divide the tuna mixture into 8 portions. Shape each portion into a fish by first forming a ¾-inch-thick oval pattie, then lightly pressing to shape one end into a tail.

1 **slightly beaten egg**
1 **tablespoon water**
24 **rich round crackers, finely crushed (about 1 cup)**

● In a shallow dish combine egg and water. In another shallow dish place the crushed crackers. First dip fish patties into egg mixture, then into crumbs, as shown below. Cover and chill up to 8 hours till serving time.

4 **pimiento-stuffed *or* pitted ripe olives, halved**
 Tartar sauce

● To serve, place fish patties on a greased baking sheet. Bake in a 375° oven for 15 to 20 minutes or till heated through. Place an olive half on each head for an *eye*. Serve with tartar sauce. Makes 8 servings.

Going fishin'? Make these little fish patties the catch-of-the-day at your next fishing party.

Here's a fishin' game to carry out the party theme: Tie a piece of string to a long wooden dowel and a clothespin to the end of the string. Have a curtain set up with someone in the back. As the kids throw their fishing lines over the curtain, attach small plastic bags containing water with goldfish. When the bag is attached, give the string a little jerk. After the fish are caught, have the kids transfer their goldfish to a jar for easy carrying.

After shaping the patties into fish, dip them into the egg mixture and then into the cracker crumbs.

Hobo-Style Dinner

1 pound fully cooked boneless ham, cut into ¾-inch cubes, *or* 1 pound frankfurters, quartered
2 16-ounce cans pork and beans in tomato sauce
2 tablespoons brown sugar
2 tablespoons molasses
1 teaspoon minced dried onion
½ teaspoon dry mustard

● In a large mixing bowl combine ham or frankfurters, beans, brown sugar, molasses, dried onion, and mustard. Turn mixture into an ungreased 12x7½x2-inch baking dish. Cover and chill till serving time.

1 package (10) refrigerated buttermilk biscuits

● To serve, remove cover from baking dish. Bake in a 450° oven for 20 to 25 minutes or till bubbly, stirring once.

Arrange the biscuits over the top of the hot bean mixture. Bake for 6 to 8 minutes more or till the biscuits are golden brown. Cool about 5 minutes before serving. Makes 10 servings.

For a hobo party, ask each kid to come dressed as a hobo. To continue the theme, play "Beggar." Give each child five coupons. Then have the kids take turns begging each other for their coupons. Whoever cracks a smile, loses a coupon. When everyone has taken a turn, the child with the most coupons becomes hobo king or queen and gets a hobo packsack.

For the hobo packsack, wrap treats and prizes in a bandanna. Then tie the bandanna onto a wooden dowel.

3-2-1— It's a Party Countdown

Planning is the secret to a successful party. Once everything is thought out, your party will not only run smoothly, but you'll also have fewer pre-party jitters. To help guide you in your planning, follow this easy-to-use checklist.

☐ **One Month Ahead:** The first step begins with deciding on the date, time, place, theme, and number of guests for your party. If necessary, make arrangements for hiring entertainers, renting party rooms, or planning mini trips.

☐ **Two Weeks Ahead:** Either phone or mail the invitations. If you're mailing the invitations, be sure to ask for a R.S.V.P. so that you'll know exactly how many kids will be coming.

Also make plans for the menu, activities, prizes, party favors, and decorations.

☐ **One Week Ahead:** Make or purchase the party favors, prizes, and decorations.

If you've made any special arrangements, check on the final plans.

☐ **Two or Three Days Ahead:** Double-check the final guest list and make a tentative schedule for what you'll be doing at the party.

☐ **One Day Ahead:** Plan your timetable for cooking. Try to prepare ahead as many foods as possible. Also, put together take-home bags, if you're giving them.

Clear an area for games and refreshments. Be sure the party area is safe for kids.

☐ **Party Day:** Finish making the food according to your timetable.

Set the table and put up the decorations. Place favors, take-home bags, and prizes in a convenient spot.

House-to-House Halloween

A knock at your door—the witches, goblins, and ghosts have arrived. It's Halloween! And there's no better way to celebrate than with a progressive party. Get together with your neighbors or friends to plan the fun. Begin the journey with a warm meal of Witch's Spell, Corny-Meal Muffins, Pumpkin Patch Cookies, and Spook 'n' Cider. Then proceed to the second, third, and fourth house for an evening full of games and treats. (See recipes and tips, pages 40 to 43.)

MENU
Witch's Spell
Corny-Meal Muffins
Pumpkin Patch Cookies
Spook 'n' Cider

TREATS
Roasted Pumpkin Seeds
Popcorn Logs
Goblins' Gorp

Witch's Spell

Pictured on pages 38 and 39.

6 14½-ounce cans
  chicken broth
4 medium carrots, thinly
  sliced
2 medium cooking apples,
  peeled, cored, and
  chopped (about
  2 cups)
½ cup chopped celery
½ cup chopped green pepper
1 teaspoon dried thyme,
  crushed

● In a medium Dutch oven combine broth, carrots, apples, celery, green pepper, and thyme. Bring mixture to boiling, then reduce heat. Cover and simmer for 10 minutes.

1 12-ounce package frozen
  diced cooked chicken
  (3 cups)
1 cup alphabet pasta

● Stir in chicken and pasta. Bring to boiling again, then reduce heat. Cover and simmer about 10 minutes more or till vegetables and pasta are tender. Makes 16 servings.

Corny-Meal Muffins

2 beaten eggs
1 8¾-ounce can cream-style
  corn
⅓ cup milk
¾ cup shredded cheddar
  cheese (3 ounces)
2 7- *or* 8½-ounce packages
  corn muffin mix

● Grease muffin pans or line with paper bake cups. Set pans aside.
  In a medium mixing bowl combine eggs, corn, and milk. Stir in cheese. Add dry muffin mix and stir till moistened (batter should be lumpy).

● Fill each cup two-thirds full. Bake in a 400° oven for 15 to 20 minutes or till a wooden toothpick comes out clean and the tops are slightly golden. Cool muffins in the pans for 5 minutes. If necessary, loosen carefully with a knife. Remove muffins from pans. Serve warm or cool completely. Makes 16 servings.

MENU COUNTDOWN
2 days ahead:
House 2—Begin to prepare Roasted Pumpkin Seeds.
1 day ahead:
House 1—Bake Pumpkin Patch Cookies. Store in a covered container.
House 2—Finish preparing and packaging Roasted Pumpkin Seeds.
House 3—Prepare and wrap Popcorn Logs.
House 4—Prepare and package Goblins' Gorp.
Several hours ahead:
House 1—Decorate cookies.
  Prepare Spook 'n' Cider. Cover and chill.
About 1 hour ahead:
House 1—Begin to prepare Witch's Spell.
  Prepare Corny-Meal Muffins.
Just before serving:
House 1—Heat Spook 'n' Cider.
After supper:
House 2—Have a pumpkin race giving Roasted Pumpkin Seeds as treats.
House 3—Create a mystery, giving Popcorn Logs as treats.
House 4—Have a goblin hunt giving Goblins' Gorp as treats.

Pumpkin Patch Cookies

Pictured on pages 38 and 39.

3½ cups all-purpose flour 1 teaspoon baking powder	● In a medium mixing bowl stir together flour and baking powder. Set flour mixture aside.
1½ cups butter *or* margarine ¼ teaspoon orange paste food coloring 1 cup sugar	● In a large mixer bowl beat butter or margarine and food coloring with an electric mixer on medium speed till butter is softened and food coloring is blended in (about 30 seconds). Add sugar and beat till fluffy.
1 egg 1 teaspoon vanilla	● Add egg and vanilla, then beat well. Stir in flour mixture. *Do not chill dough.*
	● Put the flower plate onto a cookie press. Pack dough, half at a time, into the cookie press. Press dough into flowers on ungreased cookie sheets.
	● Bake in a 400° oven for 7 to 8 minutes or till cookies are just light brown around edges. Remove cookies to a wire rack, then cool completely.
1 cup creamy chocolate frosting *(use Chocolate Butter Frosting on page 8 or a creamy fudge frosting mix for a 1-layer cake)* 18 green jelly beans, cut crosswise in half	● Spread the flat side of *half* of the cookies with some frosting. Top with remaining cookies to form pumpkins. For stems, attach one jelly bean half to the top of each cookie with frosting. Let stand for 1 to 2 hours or till frosting is slightly dry. Makes 36.

As the kids arrive, keep them busy by having them make their own treat bags. They can color small paper bags, then staple on orange or black strips of construction paper for easy-carrying handles. And for their first treat, slip a few *Pumpkin Patch Cookies* into each bag.

Spook 'n' Cider

10 cups apple cider *or* apple
    juice
1 12-ounce package frozen
    red raspberries
    (lightly sweetened)
5 inches stick cinnamon

● In a large saucepan combine apple cider or juice, raspberries, and cinnamon. Bring to boiling, then reduce heat. Cover and simmer for 10 minutes. Remove mixture from heat.
    Strain berries and cinnamon from mixture through a piece of cheesecloth. Cover till serving time.

● To serve, heat cider mixture till warm. Makes 16 (5-ounce) servings.

Boo! You can create a spooky sight by filling jack-o'-lanterns with dry ice and a little water—vapor will float out of the jack-o'-lantern.
    When using the dry ice, be sure that you're in a well ventilated area and protect your hands by wearing heavy gloves.

Roasted Pumpkin Seeds

4¼ cups raw pumpkin seeds
2 tablespoons cooking oil
1 teaspoon salt

● Rinse pumpkin seeds in water till pulp and strings are washed off, then drain.
    In a medium mixing bowl combine pumpkin seeds, cooking oil, and salt. Spread mixture onto a waxed-paper-lined 15x10x1-inch baking pan. Let stand for 24 to 48 hours or till dry, stirring occasionally.

● Remove waxed paper from baking pan. Toast seeds in a 325° oven for 40 minutes, stirring once or twice. Drain seeds on paper towels.

16 small clear plastic bags *or*
    6-inch-square pieces
    of colored cellophane
    wrap
    Ribbon

● Package ¼ cup of the seeds in each bag or place seeds in the center of cellophane wrap, then bring up edges. Tie closed with the ribbon. Makes 16 (¼-cup) servings.

Plan on using the seeds from about four pumpkins for this recipe. If you don't have enough, ask your friends to share the seeds from their pumpkins with you.

Use this crunchy snack for prizes in a pumpkin race. Divide the kids into two groups. Give each group a pumpkin and have the kids race by rolling the pumpkin with their feet, hands, or noses.

Popcorn Logs

14 cups popped popcorn	● Remove all unpopped kernels from popped corn. Place popcorn in a greased 17x12x2-inch baking pan. Keep popcorn warm in a 300° oven while making syrup mixture.
1 cup sugar **½ cup water** **½ cup light molasses** **¼ teaspoon salt**	● Butter the sides of a heavy 2-quart saucepan. In the saucepan combine sugar, water, molasses, and salt. Cook over medium-high heat till boiling, stirring constantly. Reduce heat to medium. Clip a candy thermometer to the side of the pan. 　Continue cooking over medium heat, stirring occasionally, till thermometer registers 250° (hard-ball stage), watching carefully to prevent the syrup from boiling over.
1 cup sunflower nuts	● Pour syrup mixture over popcorn. Add sunflower nuts and stir gently to coat popcorn. Cool mixture until easy to handle. Use buttered hands to shape mixture into sixteen 3½-inch logs. Cool logs completely.
Clear plastic wrap *or* 　**colored cellophane wrap** **Ribbon**	● Wrap each log in clear plastic or colored cellophane wrap. Tie ends closed with ribbon. Makes 16 servings.

Get your guests involved in creating a mystery. First gather everyone in a circle. Dim the lights, but keep the jack-o'-lanterns lit. Then start by making up a mystery tale. But before you finish it, turn to the child next to you and have him add onto the story. Continue adding onto the mystery until everyone has taken a turn.

Goblins' Gorp

3½ cups honey graham cereal **1½ cups peanuts** **1½ cups raisins** **1½ cups candy-coated milk** 　**chocolate pieces**	● In a large mixing bowl combine honey graham cereal, peanuts, raisins, and chocolate pieces.
16 small clear plastic bags *or* 　**12-inch-square pieces** 　**of colored cellophane** 　**wrap** **Ribbon**	● Package ½ cup of the mixture in each bag or place mixture in the center of the cellophane wrap, then bring up edges. Tie closed with ribbon. Makes 16 (½-cup) servings.

When the little ones come to your house, have a goblin hunt. Draw small pictures of goblins on paper and attach them to a treat. Then hide the packages. When all of the treats are found, send the kids to the next house.

Fill-Your-Pocket Pitas

What's to eat? Here's an easy and fun way to answer that question at your next party—have everyone open up their "pockets" (pocket bread, that is) and fill them full of edible coins, sticks, and other stuff from our mix-and-match chart. Plan on about 1½ ounces of meat and cheese for each pocket.

● Plan on *1 large pita bread round* for every *2* guests. Cut pita bread rounds crosswise in half. Open each bread half to form a pocket. Put bread into a plastic bag and close till serving time.
● Put spreads in individual containers. Cover and chill spreads, except for the butter or margarine, till serving time.
● Cut cold cut slices into quarters.
● Cut cheese into julienne sticks.
● Arrange cold cuts, vegetables, and cheese on a platter or in individual containers. Cover and chill till serving time.
● At serving time, set out all of the ingredients. Let guests make their own sandwiches by first spreading the inside of a pita pocket with one of the spreads, then filling it with cold cuts, veggie coins, green stuff, and cheese sticks.

Spreads	+ Cold Cut Liners	+ Veggie Coins	+ Green Stuff
Mayonnaise *or* salad dressing	Sliced bologna	Thinly sliced carrots	Torn lettuce
Soft-style cream cheese	Sliced turkey *or* chicken breast	Sliced cucumber *or* zucchini	Thinly sliced celery
Butter *or* margarine, softened	Sliced boiled ham, honey loaf, *or* salami	Cherry tomatoes, cut in half	Chopped green pepper
		Pickle slices	Alfalfa sprouts

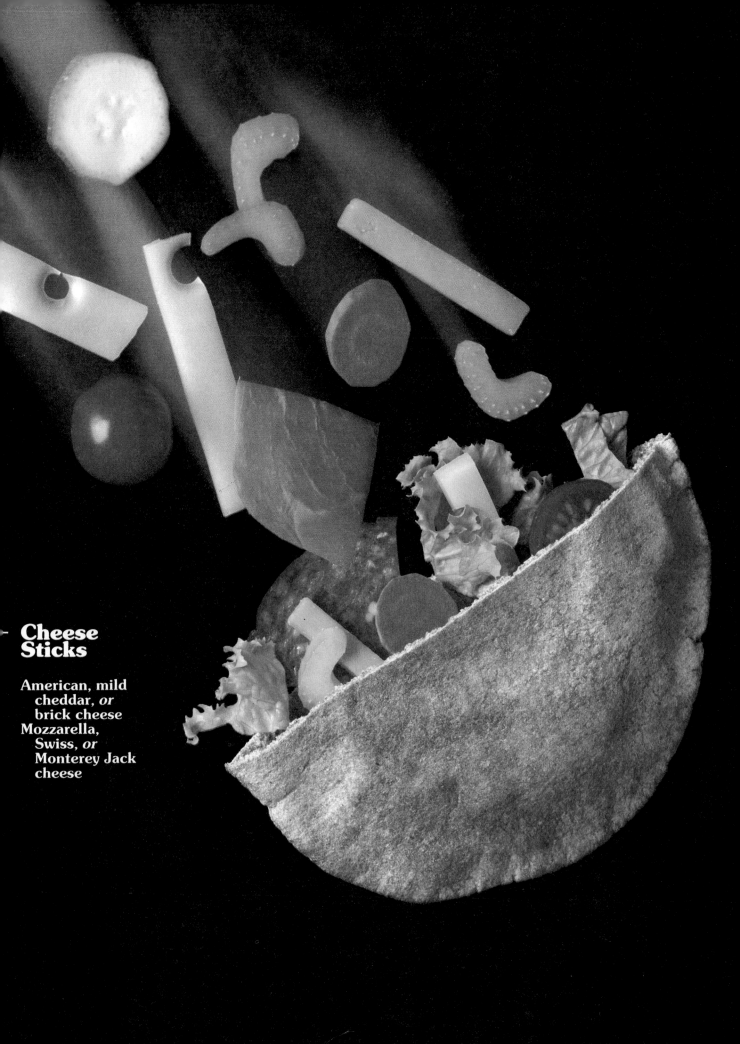

Cheese Sticks

American, mild
  cheddar, *or*
  brick cheese
Mozzarella,
Swiss, *or*
Monterey Jack
cheese

Barbecued Beef Boats

1 pound ground beef
¼ cup chopped onion
¼ cup chopped green pepper
¼ cup chopped celery
¾ cup catsup
⅓ cup water
1 tablespoon brown sugar
1 tablespoon lemon juice
1 tablespoon Worcestershire sauce
¼ teaspoon dry mustard

● For filling, in a 10-inch skillet cook ground beef, onion, green pepper, and celery till beef is brown and vegetables are tender. Drain off fat.

Stir in catsup, water, brown sugar, lemon juice, Worcestershire sauce, and dry mustard. Bring mixture to boiling, then reduce heat. Simmer, uncovered, about 5 minutes or till slightly thickened. Cover and chill till serving time.

8 French-style rolls (about 4 inches long)
2 slices American cheese, diagonally quartered (2 ounces)

● Cut a lengthwise slice from the top third of each roll. Hollow out the bottom of each roll, leaving a ½-inch-thick shell. Place shells in a clear plastic bag till serving time. Reserve the bread from the inside of the shells and the top slices for another use.

For sails, spear each cheese triangle with a wooden toothpick. Cover and chill till serving time.

● To serve, heat filling till warm. Fill bread shells with about *¼ cup* of filling. Place one cheese sail upright in filling. Serve immediately. Makes 8 servings.

Let everyone share in the fun of receiving presents with a gift exchange. Before the day of the party, ask each guest to make a special present for someone else who will be at the party. The presents can be funny or pretty. Then, during the gift exchange, have each kid tell why he or she made that particular present.

Party Helpers

Planning a party can be as much fun as giving it. But to get your party off the ground, you'll have to choose a theme, send out invitations, make the food, and put up decorations. Where can you find the help you need? The answer isn't far away—just ask your young host or hostess to pitch in.

Obviously, younger kids will be less involved in the party planning than older kids. Yet younger kids can still enjoy helping you shop, stuffing take-home bags, and decorating invitations.

Once the kids get older, they can take on the tasks of addressing invitations, making decorations and name tags, planning games and prizes, setting the table, and helping with simple recipes.

Taco Terrific Burgers

2 slightly beaten eggs
2 teaspoons Worcester-
  shire sauce
1½ teaspoons chili powder
1 teaspoon sugar
1 teaspoon prepared
  mustard
½ teaspoon garlic salt
½ cup finely crushed tortilla
  chips (about 2 cups
  uncrushed)
2 pounds ground beef

● In a medium mixing bowl combine eggs, Worcestershire sauce, chili powder, sugar, mustard, and garlic salt. Stir in crushed chips. Add beef and mix well.

● Shape meat mixture into eight ½-inch-thick patties. Place patties in a 15x10x1-inch baking pan. Cover with foil and chill till serving time.

8 lettuce leaves
1 4-ounce package shredded
  cheddar cheese (1 cup)
4 large pita bread rounds,
  halved crosswise
  Chopped tomato, mild
  taco sauce, *or* catsup

● To serve, bake patties, covered, in a 350° oven for 30 to 35 minutes or to desired doneness. Place a lettuce leaf, some cheese, and a burger into each pita bread pocket. Top with chopped tomato, taco sauce, or catsup. Makes 8 servings.

● **Barbecue method:** Grill patties, on an uncovered grill, directly over *medium-hot* coals for 7 minutes. Turn and grill patties for 6 to 8 minutes more or to desired doneness.

Make this Mexican flavored burger the star at an around-the-world party. For the invitations, make little globes by cutting out circles of paper and drawing countries on them. Ask the kids to dress in the costume of any country they choose. For added fun, plan activities with an international origin, such as breaking a piñata (see tip, page 67).

Nutty-Nutbread Sandwiches

1 **cup peanut butter** 1 **tablespoon honey** 1 **ripe medium banana, mashed** ¼ **cup chopped pitted dates**	● In a small mixing bowl combine peanut butter, honey, banana, and chopped dates.

2 **7-ounce cans date and nut
    roll**
	● Slice *each* date and nut roll into 16 slices. Spread *half* of the bread slices with the peanut butter mixture, then top with the remaining slices.
	    Wrap sets of 2 sandwiches in clear plastic wrap. Makes 8 servings.

Invite your friends over for a lets-be-nuts party! Cut out nut-shape invitations and decorations. For games, you can have a nut hunt or play "Drop the Peanut in the Bottle."

Beachside Bagelwich

1 **18-ounce jar chunk-style
    peanut butter (2 cups)**
¼ **cup honey**
⅓ **cup finely snipped dried
    fruit (raisins, dates,
    apricots, figs, *or*
    apples)**
⅓ **cup shredded carrot *or*
    zucchini, *or* finely
    chopped celery**
	● In a medium mixing bowl combine peanut butter and honey. Divide mixture into thirds. Set one-third aside.
	    Stir dried fruit into another third of the mixture. To the remaining third stir in carrot, zucchini, or celery.

48 **miniature bagels, split**	● Spread the inside of *16* bagels with *each* of the peanut butter mixtures. Place bagel sandwiches on a serving platter and cover with clear plastic wrap till serving time. Makes 16 servings.

Plan a picnic party at the beach. For each guest, tuck three of these mini bagelwiches, a small can or carton of juice, a couple of cookies, and a piece of fruit in a small plastic pail. Use clear plastic wrap and a rubber band for the cover. (Or, use covered plastic ice cream tubs.) Then let each kid tote his own lunch. After lunch see how fast the lunch pails become sand pails!

Slumber Dogs

1 16-ounce loaf frozen
   bread dough, thawed
1 1-pound package (10)
   frankfurters
   Prepared mustard
   Catsup

● Divide dough into 10 portions. On a lightly floured surface roll out each portion into a 10x2½-inch rectangle.

Place a frankfurter lengthwise on each rectangle, about ¾ inch from one end. Spread frankfurter with mustard and catsup. Fold dough over to cover ¾ of the frankfurter. Moisten edges with water. Press together to seal.

Transfer to a greased baking sheet. Cover and let dough rise in a warm place for 30 minutes.

Bake in a 375° oven for 15 to 17 minutes or till golden brown.

Perfect for your next slumber party or camping-out party—these dogs already come in their own sleeping bags. Conquer the midnight hungries by including chips or popcorn; carrot or celery sticks; and milk, juice or soda pop.

1 4⅝-ounce pressurized can
   cheddar cheese spread
   Corn snack horns
   Finely chopped green
   pepper
   Pimiento pieces

● Cool slightly. To decorate, use cheese to make hair and to attach corn snack horns as hats. Attach green pepper to frankfurter for eyes and pimiento for mouth. Makes 10 servings.

Zip-a-Dee-Zoo Party

Invite the lions, tigers, giraffes, and monkeys to your next party. You either can take this party to the zoo or make an animal wall mural at home. For a take-along party, make the sandwiches, snacks, and drink ahead of time. Pack them in a cooler. Then, when the guests arrive, all you need to do is head for the zoo. For an at-home party, just tack up a large piece of paper, draw the outlines of different animals, and let the kids color their own zoo. (See recipes, pages 52 and 53.)

MENU
Full-of-Boloney Sandwiches
Apple Sack Snacks
Jazzy Juice
Chocolate Critters

Full-of-Boloney Sandwiches

Pictured on pages 50 and 51.

12 ounces bologna, ground
   (2 cups)
¼ cup sweet pickle relish
2 tablespoons finely
   chopped onion
⅓ cup mayonnaise *or* salad
   dressing

● For filling, in a medium mixing bowl combine the ground bologna, pickle relish, and onion. Stir in mayonnaise or salad dressing.

5 slices whole wheat bread
4 slices white bread
   Small clear plastic bags

● Make 3 double-decker sandwiches by using 3 slices of the bread for each sandwich. Alternately put slices of whole wheat and white bread together with bologna mixture.
   Cut the sandwiches into fourths. Reassemble sandwiches and place in plastic bags. Close. Chill till serving time.

● For a take-along party, just before leaving home, pack the sandwiches in an insulated chest with ice packs. Makes 6 servings.

MENU COUNTDOWN
1 day ahead:
Prepare, wrap, and refrigerate Chocolate Critters.
Several hours ahead:
Prepare, wrap, and chill Full-of-Boloney Sandwiches.
   Prepare and chill Apple Sack Snacks.
   Prepare and chill the juice mixture of Jazzy Juice.
For a take-along party:
Pack picnic supplies. Just before leaving home, pack Full-of-Boloney Sandwiches, Apple Sack Snacks, and Chocolate Critters in an insulated chest with ice packs.
   Stir ginger ale into juice mixture and pour Jazzy Juice into insulated vacuum bottles.
For an at-home party:
Just before serving, stir the ginger ale into the juice mixture and pour Jazzy Juice into glasses.

Apple Sack Snacks

Pictured on pages 50 and 51.

¼ cup peanut butter
2 tablespoons chopped
   pitted dates
1 tablespoon honey

● In a small mixing bowl combine peanut butter, dates, and honey, then stir till well blended.

   Lemon juice
3 medium apples, cored and
   halved lengthwise

● Brush lemon juice onto cut surfaces of apples to prevent browning.
   Fill the center of each apple half with about *1 tablespoon* of the peanut butter mixture. Place each apple half in a paper bake cup, then put apples in a covered container. Chill till serving time.

● For a take-along party, just before leaving home, pack container of apples in an insulated chest with ice packs. Makes 6 servings.

Before planning a trip to the zoo, find out if any of your guests are afraid of animals. If so, stay close to those children to make sure they're having a good time. Spend some extra time talking to them about the animals. And for extra supervision while you're at the zoo, ask a friend to go along.

Chocolate Critters

Pictured on pages 50 and 51.

Butter *or* margarine	● Line a baking sheet with waxed paper, then grease the paper with butter or margarine. Set baking sheet aside.
½ cup butterscotch pieces ½ cup semisweet chocolate pieces ¼ cup light corn syrup 2 tablespoons butter *or* margarine 3 cups crisp rice cereal	● In a medium heavy saucepan heat butterscotch pieces, chocolate pieces, corn syrup, and butter or margarine till melted, stirring constantly. Remove from heat and stir in cereal till evenly coated. 　Turn onto prepared baking sheet and pat into a 12x6-inch rectangle. Chill about 15 minutes or till slightly firm.
Assorted decorations (red cinnamon candies, shoestring licorice, candy corn, gumdrops, candy-coated milk chocolate pieces, candied cherries, mixed dried fruit bits, *and/or* nuts)	● Cut cereal mixture into desired animal shapes with cookie cutters. Trim animals with assorted decorations. 　Chill till firm. Wrap each animal in clear plastic wrap. Chill till serving time.
	● For a take-along party, just before leaving home, pack animals in an insulated chest with ice packs. Makes 6 servings.

If there's a petting zoo in your area, take your party there. Not only can the kids pet the animals, but at some zoos, they also can feed the animals.

Jazzy Juice

Pictured on pages 50 and 51.

1 6-ounce can frozen pineapple-orange juice concentrate, thawed 1 6-ounce can frozen lemonade concentrate, thawed 1 cup water	● In a large nonmetal pitcher combine pineapple-orange juice concentrate, lemonade concentrate, and water. Cover and chill till serving time.
1 32-ounce bottle ginger ale, chilled	● For a take-along party, just before leaving home, stir ginger ale into the juice mixture and pour into insulated vacuum bottles. 　For an at-home party, to serve, stir ginger ale into juice mixture. Makes about 6 (8-ounce) servings.

To keep this drink ice-cold in insulated vacuum bottles, precool the bottles by filling them with cold tap water. Then cover the bottles and let them stand for 5 minutes. Pour out the water and fill the bottles with the juice.

Chocolate Caramel Apples

18 small apples 18 wooden sticks	● Wash and dry apples. Remove stems. Insert one wooden stick into the stem end of each apple. Set apples aside.
½ cup butter *or* margarine 2 squares (2 ounces) unsweetened chocolate 2 cups packed brown sugar 1 cup light corn syrup 1 14-ounce can (1¼ cups) *sweetened condensed* milk 1 teaspoon vanilla	● In a heavy 3-quart saucepan melt the butter or margarine and unsweetened chocolate over low heat. Add brown sugar, corn syrup, and sweetened condensed milk, then mix well. Clip a candy thermometer onto side of pan. Cook over medium heat, stirring frequently, till thermometer registers 245° (firm-ball stage). Remove saucepan from heat. Stir in vanilla.
1 cup chopped peanuts	● Dip each apple into the hot caramel mixture, using a spoon to spread the mixture evenly over apple. Allow excess caramel mixture to drip off. Immediately dip bottoms of apples into peanuts. Place apples, peanut side down, on waxed paper and let stand about 25 minutes or till firm. Makes 18.

Fruit Kabobs

8 cups assorted fruits
   (apple, pear, banana,
   peach, *or* pineapple
   chunks; strawberries;
   grapes; *and/or* mandarin
   orange sections)
   Lemon juice
30 6-inch bamboo skewers

● For kabobs, dip apple, pear, banana, and peach chunks into lemon juice to prevent them from browning. On the skewers, alternately thread fruit. Cover and chill till serving time.

For younger children, it may be easier for them to eat the fruit by putting it into bowls and letting them pick up the pieces with toothpicks.

2 8-ounce packages cream
   cheese, softened
1 8-ounce carton strawberry
   yogurt
1 7-ounce jar marshmallow
   creme

● For dip, in a mixer bowl beat cream cheese and yogurt with an electric mixer on low speed till well blended. Fold in marshmallow creme. Cover and chill till serving time.

● To serve, arrange kabobs on a platter. Serve with dip. Makes 15 servings.

Pudding Mountains

3 packages 4-serving-size
   instant pudding mix
   (any flavor)
6 cups milk
2½ cups tiny marshmallows
⅔ cup toasted coconut,
   chopped nuts, *or*
   miniature semisweet
   chocolate pieces

● Prepare pudding mix with milk according to package directions. Let stand for 5 minutes. Stir in the tiny marshmallows and coconut, nuts, or chocolate pieces. Cover and chill mixture till serving time.

If the serving size is too large for your very young guests, use half of a banana and ¼ cup of the pudding mixture.

15 small bananas, peeled
1 8-ounce container frozen
   whipped dessert
   topping, thawed
   Toasted coconut, chopped
   nuts, miniature
   semisweet chocolate
   pieces, *or* chopped
   maraschino cherries

● To serve, cut bananas *lengthwise* and *crosswise* in half. Arrange the 4 banana pieces in each serving dish. Spoon about ½ cup of the pudding mixture on top of banana. Top with some dessert topping and sprinkle with the coconut, nuts, chocolate pieces, or cherries. Serves 15.

Snow Oranges

4 medium oranges, cut crosswise in half	● Cut a thin slice of peel from the bottom of each orange half so the oranges will sit flat. Squeeze out juice, reserving ⅔ *cup*. Using a spoon, scoop out and discard the pulp and white membrane, leaving a ¼-inch-thick shell. Cover and chill till serving time.
1 cup milk **½ cup sugar**	● In a blender container or food processor bowl combine the reserved orange juice, milk, and sugar, then cover and blend or process till combined. Pour into a 9x9x2-inch pan, then freeze for 2 to 3 hours or till firm.
1 4-ounce container frozen whipped dessert topping, thawed	● Break frozen mixture into large chunks and place them into a mixer bowl. Beat with an electric mixer on low speed for 1 to 2 minutes or till chunks are broken into smaller pieces. Beat on medium speed for 4 to 5 minutes or till smooth. Fold dessert topping into beaten mixture, then return to the pan and freeze till firm.
8 maraschino cherries (optional)	● To serve, mound frozen mixture into orange shells. If desired, top with maraschino cherries. Makes 8 servings.

Our kid tasters thought the orange cups made the "snow" fun to eat. To make the cups extra special, cut the edges into scallops or into a sawtooth pattern.

Fruit 'n' Yogurt

1 17-ounce can fruit cocktail, drained **1 medium banana, sliced** **1 medium apple, cored and chopped** **½ cup tiny marshmallows**	● In a bowl combine fruit cocktail, banana, apple, and marshmallows.
1 8-ounce carton lemon *or* vanilla yogurt **2 tablespoons sifted powdered sugar**	● In a small bowl combine yogurt and sugar. Stir into fruit mixture. Cover and chill at least 2 hours before serving. Makes 8 servings.

By using a muffin pan as a serving tray, you can serve this dessert lickety-split. Just line the pan with foil bake cups. Then fill each with some of the dessert.

Build-Your-Own Sundae

Here's the master plan: You supply the ingredients (your favorites from our list) and let your guests build themselves a towering sundae. For the younger kids, limit the number of ingredient choices. (Perhaps choose only two of the options in each category.) And plan on using about ½ cup of ice cream and ⅓ cup of fruit for each sundae. But for the older kids, you may need to double or even triple the choices and amounts!

● Prepare Choco-Mallow Sauce and Blueberry Sauce. Cover and chill until party time.
● Place scoops of each kind of ice cream into individual large, chilled serving bowls. Cover and freeze till serving time.
● Put sauces and sprinkles in individual containers. Cover till serving time. Chill sauces till party time.
● At party time, set out sauces, sprinkles, and sundae dishes.
   Peel, remove pits, and slice nectarines. Peel and slice bananas. Dip nectarine and banana slices into *lemon juice* to prevent browning. If necessary, slice any large whole strawberries. Put fruit in individual containers. Cover till serving time.
● At serving time, remove covers from containers of ingredients. Set out ice cream. Let guests make their own sundaes by first placing some sauce in a dish, then ice cream and fruit. Top with more sauce and some sprinkles.

Sauces

Choco-Mallow Sauce *(see recipe at right)*

Blueberry Sauce *(see recipe at right)*

Caramel topping

Honey

Ice Cream + Fruit + Sprinkles

Ice Cream

Vanilla *or* butter pecan ice cream

Strawberry ice cream

Chocolate ice cream

Fruit

Nectarines *or* canned peach slices, drained

Bananas

Fresh strawberries *or* frozen unsweetened whole strawberries, thawed

Canned pineapple tidbits, drained

Sprinkles

Granola

Chopped peanuts *or* sunflower nuts

Toasted coconut

Mixed dried fruit bits

Miniature semisweet chocolate pieces

Choco-Mallow Sauce: In a small heavy saucepan melt 1½ cups *tiny marshmallows* in ¾ cup *milk* over medium heat. After marshmallows are melted, add one 6-ounce package (1 cup) *semisweet chocolate pieces*. Continue heating and stirring with a wire whisk till chocolate is melted. Remove from heat and cool slightly. Pour mixture into a serving dish. Cover and chill. At party time, set sauce out to bring to room temperature. Makes 2 cups.

Blueberry Sauce: In a small saucepan combine 2 cups fresh *or* frozen *blueberries,* 3 tablespoons *orange juice,* and 2 tablespoons *sugar.* Cook and stir over medium heat till mixture is bubbly. Remove from heat and coarsely crush the blueberries. Cool slightly. Pour mixture into a serving dish. Cover and chill. At party time, set sauce out to bring to room temperature. Makes 1½ cups.

Fruity Juice Pops

Pictured opposite.

1 3-ounce package orange-, concord grape-, *or* strawberry-flavored gelatin
1 cup boiling water
1 6-ounce can frozen orange *or* grape juice concentrate, *or* red Hawaiian fruit punch concentrate
3 cups water

● In a medium bowl dissolve gelatin in boiling water. Add frozen concentrate. Stir till melted. Stir in water.

When a child's best friend is moving away, why not have one last celebration together at a neighborhood block party? Both kids and adults will enjoy the fun of water balloon or egg tosses, softball, and tug-of-war.

15 3-ounce paper cups
15 wooden sticks

● Pour about *⅓ cup* of juice mixture into each paper cup.
  Cover each cup with foil. Make a small hole in the center of foil. Insert a stick through the hole into the juice mixture. Freeze about 5 hours or till firm.
  To serve, let pops stand at room temperature about 5 minutes; peel paper cups off pops. Makes 15 pops.

Hawaiian Pops

1 envelope unflavored gelatin
1 9-ounce can cream of coconut

● In a small saucepan soften gelatin in cream of coconut. Place saucepan over low heat and stir till gelatin is dissolved. Cool gelatin mixture about 10 minutes.

Even if you don't live in Hawaii, you still can carry on the festivities of a luau in your own backyard with a cookout or swimming party. For an islandlike atmosphere, play Hawaiian music, wear paper leis, and make grass skirts by cutting 1-inch-wide slits in plastic garbage bags.

1 6-ounce can frozen pineapple juice concentrate, thawed
2½ cups water
12 3-ounce paper cups
12 wooden sticks

● Stir pineapple juice concentrate and water into gelatin mixture.
  Pour about *⅓ cup* of juice mixture into each paper cup.
  Cover each cup with foil. Make a small hole in the center of foil. Insert a stick through the hole into the juice mixture. Freeze about 5 hours or till firm.
  To serve, let pops stand at room temperature about 5 minutes; peel paper cups off pops. Makes 12 pops.